KOSOVO 2016 HUMAN RIGHTS REPORT

EXECUTIVE SUMMARY

Kosovo is a parliamentary democracy. The constitution and laws provide for an elected unicameral parliament, which in turn elects a president, whose choice of prime minister the parliament must approve. The country last held parliamentary elections in June 2014, which international observers considered free and fair. Parliament elected Hashim Thaci as president on February 26; his inauguration was on April 8. The EU's Rule-of-Law Mission (EULEX), which monitors police and the justice sector, continued to perform some executive functions, with its mission extended until 2018. The EU-facilitated Brussels Dialogue on the normalization of relations between Kosovo and Serbia continued. Northern Kosovo judicial structures have yet to be integrated into the national structures following the 2015 justice-sector agreement between Kosovo and Serbia.

Civilian authorities maintained effective control of the security forces.

One of the most serious human rights problems was the occasionally violent obstruction of parliament by opposition deputies, blocking free debate and the passage of legislation. Endemic government and private-sector corruption coupled with the lack of punishment for corrupt acts remained an important human rights problem. Societal violence and institutional discrimination against members of some religious communities; ethnic minorities; women; persons with disabilities; and members of the lesbian, gay, bisexual, transgender, and intersex (LGBTI) community constituted a third significant area of concern.

Other human rights problems included: reported police mistreatment of detainees; substandard physical conditions combined with drug abuse, corruption, and favoritism in prisons; lengthy pretrial detention and judicial inefficiency resulting in mistrials; and unresolved property restitution claims from the 1998-99 war. There was also intimidation of media by public officials, foreign governments, and criminal elements; restriction of freedom of movement across the Austerlitz Bridge; and violence against displaced persons seeking to return to their homes and those who had already returned. Restrictions on religious freedom included the lack of a registration system, the repeated vandalism of religious property, and restrictions on freedom of worship for Serbian Orthodox pilgrims. Additional human rights problems included domestic violence and discrimination against women; gender-biased sex selection; child abuse; trafficking in persons; discrimination against ethnic minorities, especially Ashkalis, Egyptians, and

Roma; inadequate support for persons with disabilities; poor conditions in mental health facilities; sporadic ethnic tensions; and child labor in the informal economy.

The government took steps to prosecute and punish officials who committed abuses in the security services or elsewhere in the government. Many in the opposition, civil society, and the media assumed that senior officials engaged in corruption with impunity.

In its February 26 report, the UN Human Rights Advisory Panel (UNHRAP) criticized the UN Mission in Kosovo (UNMIK) for its handling of mass lead poisoning of displaced Roma who were moved into contaminated camps immediately following the war in 1999. UNHRAP faulted UNMIK's unwillingness to follow the panel's guidance, resulting in the absence of redress for complainants.

Section 1. Respect for the Integrity of the Person, Including Freedom from:

a. Arbitrary Deprivation of Life and other Unlawful or Politically Motivated Killings

There were no reports that the government or its agents committed arbitrary or unlawful killings.

EULEX and domestic prosecutors continued prosecuting war crimes cases arising from the 1998-99 conflict. While EULEX investigated war crimes, it transferred other cases which had not reached trial to local special prosecutors.

In September a EULEX-majority panel of judges at the country's Appellate Court rendered final verdicts in the Drenica I and II war crimes cases. The cases included 15 defendants tried for practical reasons in groups of seven and 10 defendants, respectively, with two of the same defendants in both.

The Appellate Court largely upheld the May 2015 Basic Court of Mitrovice/Mitrovica's verdict in the Drenica I case, convicting three and acquitting four defendants. The Appellate Court upheld the conviction of the former ambassador to Albania, Sylejman Selimi, but reduced his sentence to six years and three months. It acquitted the serving mayor of Skenderaj/Srbica, Sami Lushtaku, of murder. It overturned his previous acquittal for command responsibility for war crimes committed against civilians in a Kosovo Liberation Army (KLA) detention center and sentenced him to seven years. Lushtaku's conviction was not final, given the reversal of his acquittal. On November 29, his attorney announced the filing of an appeal with the Supreme Court, noting the conviction was based on the testimony of only one witness. The court upheld the acquittals of Sahit Jashari, Ismet Haxha, Avni Zabeli, Jahir Demaku, and Sabit Geci.

The Appellate Court upheld the original May 2015 conviction of all 10 defendants in the Drenica II case, but reduced some prison terms, sentencing Sylejman Selimi to seven instead of eight years, Isni Thaci to six and a half years instead of seven, and sentencing Jahir Demaku and Zeqir Demaku to six years instead of seven. The Appellate Court confirmed the sentences of three years for parliament member Fadil Demaku, Gllogovc/Glogovac Mayor Nexhat Demaku, and Agim, Driton, Bashkim, and Selman Demaj. Fadil Demaku and Nexhat Demaku's respective parliamentary mandates were forfeited. The Appellate Court issued Sylejman Selimi and Jahir Demaku, named in both cases, with aggregate sentences of 10 and seven years, respectively. On March 16, Minister of Justice Hajredin Kuci criticized EULEX judges for their decision in the case, calling the EULEX verdict "unjust and absurd" and claiming there was no evidence on which to base a conviction. He expressed confidence that the Court of Appeals would make the "right decision" in this case. EULEX noted the statement could be perceived as intimidation and political interference.

On January 21, a trial panel of EULEX judges at the Basic Court in Mitrovice/Mitrovica convicted Oliver Ivanovic, leader of the Serbia, Democracy, and Justice party of war crimes against civilians and sentenced him to nine years in prison. The court found Ivanovic had encouraged the murder of Kosovo-Albanians by Serb paramilitary forces in 1999. The panel acquitted him of the charge of attempted aggravated murder. The panel heard Ivanovic's appeal on October 11; as of November 7, it continued to review evidence and testimony.

On May 17, a EULEX-majority panel of the Basic Court of Pristina convicted Enver Sekiraqa and sentenced him to 37 years in prison for inciting the 2007 murder of police officer Triumf Riza. Arben Berisha was previously convicted and serving a 35-year sentence for the crime.

Convicted war criminal Sabit Geci returned to Dubrava prison following an August 12 decision by the Minister of Justice Dhurate Hoxha that ordered all convicted prisoners on extended medical leave to return to correctional facilities. The Ministry of Justice previously suspended Geci's sentence in October 2015. Geci was found guilty in 2011 of war crimes committed at detention centers in northern Albania and was serving a 15-year and 12-year sentences, respectively.

The EU's 2016 report stated that the country had fulfilled its remaining obligations related to the establishment of the Specialist Chambers and Specialist Prosecution Office to investigate allegations of international crimes committed during and after the 1999 conflict. On September 5, the EU announced David Schwendiman, the lead prosecutor of the EU's Special Investigative Task Force (SITF), would serve as the specialist prosecutor (chief prosecutor) of the newly established Kosovo specialist prosecutor's office (SPO). Schwendiman was appointed pursuant to the 2015 Kosovo Law on Specialist Chambers and Specialist Prosecutor's Office. His appointment marked the formal transition of the former SITF into the independent SPO. The SPO is an independent office for the investigation and prosecution of the crimes within the jurisdiction of the Specialist Chambers, which can issue indictments and try cases, as appropriate, resulting from the evidentiary findings of the SITF. The SITF was established after the 2011 release of the Council of Europe (CoE) report, *Inhuman Treatment of People and Illicit Trafficking in Human Organs in Kosovo*, on alleged crimes committed by individual KLA leaders during and just after the Kosovo war. The mandate of the SITF is to investigate and, if warranted, prepare cases for prosecution involving serious crimes alleged in the CoE report, including war crimes and organized crimes. The law creating the Specialist Chambers foresaw the creation of a specialist prosecutor's office with the authority to indict suspects and provides for some proceedings to take place elsewhere in Europe.

On October 17, the Dutch Parliament ratified the February 15 Host State Agreement for the Specialist Chambers, which was ratified by then president Atifete Jahjaga on February 29. As of November 7, a number of organizational steps remained to be completed, including the selection of judges, before Specialist Prosecutor David Schwendiman could finalize charges and file indictments.

b. Disappearance

There were no reports of politically motivated disappearances, abductions, or kidnappings.

As of November the International Committee of the Red Cross (ICRC) listed as missing 1,660 persons who disappeared during the 1998-99 conflict and the political violence that followed. Although the ICRC did not distinguish missing persons by ethnic background due to confidentiality restrictions, observers suggested that approximately 70 percent were ethnic Albanians and 30 percent were Serbs, Roma, Ashkalis, Egyptians, Bosniaks, and Montenegrins.

Efforts to recover remains continued with limited results. According to the ICRC, 14 missing persons' cases were closed during the year, including seven new identifications, two persons located alive, and five cases closed based on a revision of their files. According to the ICRC, six new missing persons' cases were opened during the year. The government's Commission on Missing Persons reported that, as of October, EULEX and the government's Institute of Forensic Medicine conducted 11 field operations and exhumations. Authorities recovered remains from known gravesites that could lead to the identification of additional missing persons. Seven field operations at new sites did not yield any remains, including two in majority-Serb northern municipalities. Based on a prosecutor's order, an excavation was undertaken at the University of Pristina campus in July, but no human remains were recovered. The government invited forensic experts from Serbia to observe the excavation, which they did. Likewise, the country's forensic experts observed an excavation in Kizevak at the invitation of the Serbian government; however, works at this site were not yet concluded.

The ICRC-chaired working group on persons unaccounted for in relation to the events in Kosovo in the 1998-2000 period continued to meet, exchanging information and records to help elucidate the fate of the missing. The government's delegation continued to request a change in the working group's terms of reference to remove UNMIK from its delegation, to reflect the country's independence.

As of October the International Commission on Missing Persons received 45 samples from the Institute of Forensic Medicine, resulting in seven new DNA matches. Remains were identified in 38 cases and were re-associated with remains from previously resolved cases.

c. Torture and Other Cruel, Inhuman, or Degrading Treatment or Punishment

The law prohibits such practices, but there were some reports that government officials employed them.

The Police Inspectorate of Kosovo (PIK), an independent body within the Ministry of Internal Affairs, was responsible for reviewing complaints about police behavior. As of November PIK reviewed 1,246 citizen complaints regarding police conduct. PIK characterized 748 of these as disciplinary violations and forwarded them to the Kosovo Police Professional Standards Unit; PIK judged another 493 complaints to be criminal cases. As of November, 179 police personnel were under investigation, while another 12 cases from 2015 remained under investigation. Allegations of excessive use of force by police in dispersing a demonstration in January 2015 did not result in criminal charges, although prosecutors continued to review information provided by PIK.

On August 8, the Basic Court in Mitrovica convicted a former Kosovo Liberation Army (KLA) commander, Xhemshit Krasniqi, for the arrest, illegal detention, violation of bodily integrity and health, and torture of several witnesses and unknown civilians, carried out in 1999 at KLA camps in Kukes and Cahan in Albania as well as in Prizren in Kosovo.

Prison and Detention Center Conditions

Prison and detention center conditions generally met international standards, but significant problems persisted for prisoners in penitentiaries, specifically, the lack of rehabilitative programs, prisoner-on-prisoner violence, corruption, and substandard medical care.

On November 17, authorities indicted numerous correctional officers for enabling the escape of prisoners and not executing court orders. Notably, several senior corrections officials, including Emrush Thaci, former Director of the Pristina Detention Center, were indicted for aiding Sami Lushtaku, a convicted war criminal, who had avoided jail time with the help of corrections officials.

During the year the Kosovo Rehabilitation Center for Torture Victims (KRCT) received complaints from prisoners regarding inappropriate behavior, verbal harassment, and, in one instance, physical mistreatment by correctional officers, mainly at the Dubrava KRCT and the High Security Prison. Prosecutors opened an investigation in January, and in September the KRCT requested the prosecutor's office in Istog/Istok expedite this case.

The KRCT noted the internal complaint mechanism mandated by law did not function in prisons as inmates were not able to report human rights violations and other concerns confidentially. Prisoners in some wards at the Dubrava Prison and the High Security Prison lacked complaint forms, and prison management failed to address reported concerns. The KRCT also noted that authorities did not provide written decisions justifying solitary confinement or confirming transfer to another facility. The KRCT further stated that amendments to the 2014 Law on the Execution of Penal Sanctions were not implemented, nor were instructions for implementing the law completed, resulting in a lack of standardized procedures for leave and parole requests.

<u>Physical Conditions</u>: According to the KRCT, physical and living conditions remained substandard in some parts of the Dubrava Prison, which held 750 prisoners. Deficiencies at Dubrava included poor lighting and ventilation in some cells, dilapidated kitchens and toilets, lack of hot water, and inadequate or no bedding, as well as poor-quality renovations and significant delays in repairs.

According to the KRCT, prisoners with special needs or elderly prisoners were not housed separately within correctional institutions, and drug addicts were held with the general prison population. Two prisoners died of natural causes while in custody.

As of October the KRCT received seven complaints from prisoners that correctional staff verbally, and in some cases physically, abused them in the Dubrava Prison and the High Security Prison.

In August the KRCT reported to authorities allegations of physical abuse by prison staff of more than a dozen convicted juveniles in Lipjan/Lipljane Prison. The KRCT interviewed more than 20 juveniles at that facility who all alleged the prison staff routinely slapped detained youth. Following the complaint, the nongovernmental organization (NGO) Coalition for Protection of Juveniles visited juveniles at the Lipjan/Lipljane facility and documented numerous allegations of ill treatment. According to the KRCT, one juvenile received head injuries which were not reported to correctional authorities by medical staff.

As of October the KRCT received seven complaints from prisoners that correctional staff verbally, and in some cases physically, abused them in the Dubrava Prison and the High Security Prison.

Due to corruption and political interference, authorities did not always exercise control over the facilities or their inmates. According to the KRCT, inmates complained that officials at the Dubrava and the Smrekovnica prisons unlawfully granted furloughs and additional yard time due to nepotism or bribery. The KRCT reported that mobile phones and illicit drugs were regularly smuggled into correctional facilities, with more than 30 percent of convicts estimated to be addicted to drugs; none were enrolled in drug treatment programs.

The KRCT documented delays and errors in the delivery of medical care to prisoners as well as a lack of specialized treatment. In many instances these conditions forced prisoners to procure needed medications through private sources. The KRCT observed gaps in the prison health-care system at the Dubrava facility and reported an insufficient number of mental health professionals.

Similarly, facilities and treatment for inmates with disabilities remained substandard. The Kosovo Correctional Service held convicted prisoners with disabilities separately from the general prison population. The Kosovo Forensics Psychiatric Institute provided limited treatment and shelter for detained persons with mental disabilities. Advocates for persons with disabilities faulted the government for regularly housing pretrial detainees with diagnosed mental disabilities together with other pretrial detainees, although the Kosovo Correctional Service held pretrial detainees separately from the general prison population.

During the year the Kosovo Correctional Service established a multiprofessional team to address self-injuries and suicide attempts at correctional facilities, although advocates were not aware of improvements. The KRCT noted psychosocial services at the Dubrava Prison and High Security Prison were insufficient and unsuitable for the inmates' needs despite some improvements at the High Security Prison. There were no legal provisions or administrative instructions for the treatment of prisoners with disabilities. As of November 7, the KCRT reported 10 attempted suicides. Advocates cited frequent transfers and harsh treatment as contributing factors.

On November 5, a Vetevendosje party activist Astrit Dehari committed suicide in the Prizren Detention Center (PDC). Dehari had been detained since August 30 on terrorism charges related to an August 5 rocket-propelled grenade attack on the parliament building. On November 18, the Institute for Forensic Medicine released the final findings of an autopsy, observed by independent experts, maintaining that the cause of death was mechanical asphyxiation. Prizren District Prosecutor Syle Hoxha told media on November 6 that Dehari had scratch marks on his throat and hands. As of November 17, the complete findings of the medical examiner, including a determination of the cause of death, were not published. On November 22, the Ministry of Justice announced disciplinary measures against the acting director, two correctional supervisors, and a corrections officer at the Prizren Detention Center for improperly following procedures in the case. On November 23, authorities suspended a nurse from the detention center in Prizren in connection with the case.

<u>Administration</u>: As of August the prison population consisted of 1,515 convicts, including 52 minors and 38 women, and 334 detainees. A total of 105 foreign citizens were held: 58 convicts and 47 detainees. Officials kept records on prisoners, but correctional service administrators claimed that bureaucratic divisions of responsibility for detainees and convicts created problems. For example, prison authorities could not intervene when pretrial detainees used Ministry of Justice connections to obtain transfers to more comfortable facilities, such as the University Clinical Center in Pristina, even when the prison could provide adequate medical services. During an August 12 visit to the Clinical Center, Minister of Justice Dhurata Hoxha condemned this practice and ordered these prisoners returned to prison.

Both inmates and social workers characterized the Conditional Release Panel as failing to address requests for early release in a timely fashion and for a lack of clarity in the justification of its denials. Prisoners with good behavior records criticized the panel's lack of consideration of their individual circumstances. The Kosovo Correctional Service received 19 complaints, primarily about transfers and benefits.

<u>Independent Monitoring</u>: The government permitted visits by independent human rights observers, but the Ombudsperson Institution (OI) was the only institution that had continuous and unfettered access to correctional facilities. The KRCT and the Center for Defense of Human Rights and Freedoms (CDHRF) were required to provide 24-hour advance notice of planned monitoring activities. The OI, KRCT, and CDHRF acted as the National Preventive Mechanism, a coordinating body established to jointly monitor arrest procedures and to investigate credible allegations of inhuman prison conditions.

<u>Improvements</u>: According to the KRCT, the Kosovo Correctional Service renovated cells in some correctional institutions, including three wards of the Dubrava Prison and the kitchen at the Lipjan/Lipljane Detention Center. Authorities started assigning prisoners to the High Security Prison, which opened in 2014 in Gerdoc/Gerdovac near Podujeve/Podujevo. As of August there were 143 prisoners in the facility (130 prisoners and 13 pretrial detainees).

d. Arbitrary Arrest or Detention

The constitution and law prohibit arbitrary arrest and detention, and the government, EULEX, and Kosovo Force (KFOR), a NATO-led international peacekeeping force, generally observed these prohibitions.

Role of the Police and Security Apparatus

Local security forces included the Kosovo Police and the Kosovo Security Force (KSF). The law provides that police operate under the authority of the Ministry of Internal Affairs. Police maintained internal security, backstopped by EULEX as a second responder for incidents of unrest and KFOR as a third responder. The border police, within the Kosovo Police, were responsible for law enforcement issues related to border management.

The KSF is a lightly armed civil response force that provides disaster response and humanitarian relief, demining, search and rescue, and hazardous material containment. The Ministry for the Kosovo Security forced managed KSF.

EULEX s mandate is to monitor, mentor, and advise local judicial and law enforcement institutions. It also has some operational responsibilities, serving, with the police force as second responder, including during raids and actions requiring crowd and riot control, although it did not carry out this function during the year. EULEX's mandate for policing operations is limited to cases of organized crime, high-level corruption, war crimes, money laundering, terrorist financing, and international police cooperation. It also engaged in witness protection operations and training for police in witness protection. EULEX's executive role gradually decreased as envisaged in the exchange of letters between the government and the EU in 2014 and as extended during the year.

KFOR was tasked with providing a safe and secure environment and ensuring freedom of movement in the country. In addition to patrolling the border with Serbia, it protected the Austerlitz Bridge in Mitrovica/Mitrovice and the Serbian Orthodox Church's Visoki Decani monastery. As of October the mission comprised 4,559 troops from 31 countries.

EULEX and KFOR personnel generally operated with impunity with regard to the country's legal system but remained subject to their missions' and their countries' disciplinary measures. There were no reports of abuse by EULEX or KFOR.

The government investigated abuse and corruption, although mechanisms for doing so were not equally effective throughout the country. Local security forces in northern Kosovo transitioned to government control as part of the EU-mediated Brussels Dialogue between the country and Serbia.

Arrest Procedures and Treatment of Detainees

By law, except when a crime is in progress, police may apprehend suspects only with warrants based on evidence and issued by a judge or prosecutor. Within six hours, according to law, prosecutors must issue the arrested person a written statement describing the suspected offense and the legal basis for the charges or release the individual. Authorities must bring arrested individuals before a judge within 48 hours or release them and must provide detainees prompt access to a lawyer of their choice or one provided by the state. There is a bail system. Suspects have the right to refuse to answer questions at all stages of an investigation, except those concerning their identity. Suspects have the right to obtain the free assistance of an interpreter, and to receive medical and psychiatric treatment. Police may not hold suspects incommunicado.

Following an initial ruling, a court may hold individuals in pretrial detention for 30 days from the date of their arrest but may extend their detention for up to one year with no indictment. After an indictment and until the conclusion of trial proceedings, only a trial judge or a trial panel can order or terminate detention. The law allows a judge to order house arrest, confiscation of travel documents, and the expanded use of bail as alternatives to pretrial detention.

Although in some instances police were masked or under cover, they generally carried out arrests using warrants. There were no confirmed reports that police abused the 48-hour rule, and prosecutors generally either provided arrested persons with documents describing the reasons for their detention or released them. Officials generally respected the requirement for prompt disposition of cases, but the KRCT reported that detainees occasionally faced delays when attorneys were not available until the morning after a person's detention. The courts seldom used bail but often released detainees without bail pending trial.

NGOs reported that authorities did not always allow detained persons to contact attorneys when initially arrested and in some cases permitted consultation with an attorney only when police investigators began formal questioning. In several instances detainees were allowed access to an attorney only after their formal questioning. Some detained persons complained that despite requests for lawyers, their first contact with an attorney took place at their initial court appearance.

Pretrial Detention: Lengthy detention, both before and during judicial proceedings, remained a problem. The law allows judges to detain a defendant pending trial if there is a well-grounded suspicion that the defendant is likely to destroy, hide, or forge evidence; influence witnesses; flee; repeat the offense; engage in another criminal offense; or fail to appear at subsequent court proceedings. Judges routinely granted pretrial detention without requiring evidentiary justification. Lengthy detention was also partly due to judicial inefficiency and corruption.

<u>Detainee's Ability to Challenge Lawfulness of Detention before a Court</u>: Persons arrested or detained, regardless of whether on criminal or other grounds, are entitled to challenge in court the legal basis or arbitrary nature of their detention and obtain prompt release and compensation if found to have been unlawfully detained.

e. Denial of Fair Public Trial

The constitution provides for an independent judiciary, but the judiciary did not always provide due process. According to the European Commission, the administration of justice was slow and there was insufficient accountability for judicial officials. Judicial structures were prone to political interference, with disputed appointments and unclear mandates. According to the Kosovo Judicial Council, 417,733 civil and criminal cases awaited trial as of July. More than 95,000 actions requiring judicial decisions awaited execution, and more than 201,287 minor charges awaited adjudication.

An effective mechanism for disciplinary proceedings against judges and prosecutors was in place. Authorities generally respected court orders.

EULEX prosecutors and judges functioned as embedded members of the country's judicial system. The head of the Special Prosecutor's Office, with jurisdiction over serious crimes, including trafficking in persons, crimes against humanity, money laundering, war crimes, and terrorism, had a EULEX prosecutor as her deputy. In accordance with the 2014 exchange of letters (as extended in 2016) between the government and the EU, EULEX prosecutors may act independently or together with domestic prosecutors in compliance with applicable law. Consequently, EULEX took on some new cases and processed continuing ones.

On September 25, in a key step toward establishing formal judicial institutions in the northern municipalities, the Ministry of Justice published a list of candidates who passed the bar examination, including five Kosovo-Serb candidates who sought to be integrated into the country's justice system and start working in Mitrovica North Basic Court in accordance with the Dialogue Agreement on

Justice. As part of the continuing implementation of the dialogue with Serbia, most civil and criminal cases in the north of the country were not acted upon because the 2015 agreement on justice issues with Serbia was not yet implemented. This delay resulted in several suspects who were charged with serious crimes since 2013 being released by prosecutors in Vushtrii/Vucitrn when their cases reached the two-year statutory limit; hence, the charges were dismissed without a trial. A backlog of approximately 8,000 cases at this court and the lack of prosecutors and judges contributed to the delay of cases.

Trial Procedures

The law provides for a fair and impartial trial, and the judiciary generally upheld the law. Trials are public and the law entitles defendants to the presumption of innocence, the right to be informed promptly and in detail of charges against them, to be present at their trials, to remain silent and not to be compelled to testify or confess guilt, to confront adverse witnesses, to see evidence, and to have legal representation. Defendants have the right to appeal. These rights extend to all citizens without exception. The country does not use jury trials.

According to the Organization for Security and Cooperation in Europe, the Agency for Free Legal Aid, an independent agency mandated to provide free legal assistance to low-income individuals, has not functioned as envisioned The agency offers legal advice but does not represent cases before the court. A section of the Office of the Chief State Prosecutor helped to provide access to justice for victims of all crimes, with a special focus on victims of domestic violence, trafficking in persons, child abuse, and rape.

The Secretariat of the Kosovo Judicial Council issued a decision in January to close the country's judicial integration section that previously assisted minority communities in 11 Kosovo Serb-majority areas by accompanying them to court, filing documents with courts on their behalf, and providing information and legal assistance to refugees and displaced persons. The legal aid office in Gracanica/Gracanice closed in August, with the Kosovo Judicial Council agreeing to take custody of its legal files. Following the closure, there was no free legal aid program specifically provided by the country for the Kosovo-Serb community, although an EU-funded program started on September 26 to assist this community.

Political Prisoners and Detainees

There were no reports of political prisoners or detainees.

Civil Judicial Procedures and Remedies

There are civil remedies for human rights violations, but victims were unable to avail themselves of this recourse due to complicated bureaucratic procedures and a large backlog of judicial cases. Individuals may appeal to courts to seek damages for, or cessation of, human rights violations. In 2015 parliament approved the Law on Crime Victim Compensation, establishing a compensation program for victims of violent crimes and their dependents. The Ministry of Justice appointed a commission to review claims. As of September 14, procedures were still not in place for victims to file claims.

Individuals may turn to the Constitutional Court for review of their rights to due process. The constitution incorporates obligations agreed to in numerous international conventions as binding. Individuals may bring alleged violations of these conventions as well as violations of due process under domestic law before the Constitutional Court.

Property Restitution

The government continued to make progress toward resolving restitution of property cases. A confusing mix of laws, regulations, administrative instructions, and court practices, as well as the illegal reoccupation of properties and multiple claims for the same property, continued to hamper such cases. Private citizens as well as religious communities were largely unsuccessful in petitioning for the return of properties seized or confiscated during the Yugoslav era.

As of December 13, the Kosovo Property Claims Commission had decided 41,849 of the 42,749 registered claims for restitution, and authorities notified most claimants of results. The commission reported that the Kosovo Property Agency (KPA) authorities implemented 37,714 of its decisions. A total of 1,290 of its decisions were under appeal with the Supreme Court.

The KPA, a quasi-judicial body, had difficulty enforcing its decisions when evicting illegal occupants. The KPA also lacked funds to pay the 3.2 million euros ($3.5 million) compensation called for in the 143 claims decided in favor of persons who lost their properties in the early 1990s due to discriminatory housing practices erratically employed at that time. The agency similarly lacked funds to remove illegal structures constructed on land after claimants had their rights confirmed. As of December, the agency submitted 385 criminal charges to the

Prosecutor's Office against illegal occupants who reoccupied properties after KPA evictions; 720 eviction warrants remained pending during this period. The area of the country with the highest proportion of pending evictions was Mitrovica with 258, primarily for Kosovo Albanians.

The backlog of property claims in municipal courts remained high. Approximately 9,000 claims remained outstanding as of December 2016, most involving monetary claims by Kosovo Serbs for uninhabitable war-damaged property. The country lacked an effective system to allow Kosovo Serbs displaced from the country to file property and other claims from outside the country.

On November 19, the Law for the Kosovo Property Comparison and Verification Agency entered into force, following the Constitutional Court declaring a challenge by a Kosovo-Serb political party inadmissible. The agency's mandate includes the comparison of all cadastral documents returned from Serbia with the country's cadastral records to adjudicate claims. Claimants have the right to appeal claims in the courts.

f. Arbitrary or Unlawful Interference with Privacy, Family, Home, or Correspondence

The constitution and law prohibit such actions, and the government, EULEX, and KFOR generally respected these prohibitions.

Section 2. Respect for Civil Liberties, Including:

a. Freedom of Speech and Press

The constitution and law provide for freedom of speech and press. While the government generally respected these rights, credible reports persisted that some public officials, politicians, businesses, and radical religious groups sought to intimidate media representatives. Media also encountered difficulties in obtaining information from the government and public institutions as provided by law.

The constitution provides for an Independent Media Commission, a body whose primary responsibilities are to regulate broadcast frequencies, issue licenses to public and private broadcasters, and establish and implement broadcasting policies.

Press and Media Freedoms: Independent media were active and expressed a wide variety of views, generally without restriction, although reports persisted that government officials, some political parties, businesses connected to the government, religious groups, and disgruntled individuals exerted verbal pressure on media owners, individual editors, and reporters not to publish certain stories or materials.

Growing financial difficulties of media outlets put the editorial independence of all media at risk. While some self-sufficient media outlets adopted editorial and broadcast policies independent of political and business interests, those with fewer resources sometimes accepted financial support from various sources in exchange for positive coverage or for refraining from publishing negative stories harmful to funders' interests.

Broadcast media, particularly television channels, had more access to substantial sources of revenue than print media. The legislative assembly controlled the budget of public broadcasting station RTK and its affiliates. The public perceived private broadcasters as more independent, but smaller stations reportedly faced an increasing risk of closure and became more reliant on scarce outside funding sources. Unregulated internet media exerted further pressure on broadcast outlets by republishing articles from print or other internet sources, mostly without attribution.

<u>Violence and Harassment</u>: As of November 10, the Association of Journalists of Kosovo (AJK) and media outlets reported 17 instances in which government officials, business interests, or radical religious groups abused press freedom, including by physical assaults and verbal threats directed at journalists and pressure on outlets not to publish certain materials.

On January 26, two individuals wielding iron bars attacked Gazmend Morina, a journalist with the veriu.info web portal. Police submitted evidence to prosecutors that former Mitrovice/Mitrovica South Municipal Assemblyman Nexhat Dedia and Labinot Krasniqi attacked Morina due to his critical coverage of the Trepca mining complex, the largest mining employer in the country, and its director. As of November 10, the prosecution did not file charges or dismiss the case.

Investigative journalist Vehbi Kajtazi reported receiving a threatening text message on March 20 from Prime Minister Isa Mustafa. Kajtazi had published an article mentioning that Mustafa's brother had sought asylum in order to receive medical care. Kajtazi reported to the police that Mustafa told him "you'll pay dearly for this." Police forwarded the case to the prosecution, but as of December no charges were filed.

On July 26, media reported the Turkish Embassy filed a protest with the Foreign Ministry on July 20 demanding that authorities arrest journalist Berat Buzhala for his satirical Twitter post in response to the attempted coup d'etat in Turkey on July 15. The Association of Journalists condemned the request as scandalous and demanded an apology and the ambassador's removal. The government took no action against Buzhala.

On August 22 and August 28, hand grenades were thrown on the lawn of the public broadcaster RTK in Pristina and onto the property of RTK General Director Mentor Shala's home. The explosions caused minor damage, but no injuries; no arrests were made. An unknown group calling itself The Rugovans claimed responsibility for the attack via an e-mail sent to the media, accusing RTK of supporting the government's border demarcation agreement with Montenegro.

<u>Censorship or Content Restrictions</u>: There were no reports of direct censorship of print or broadcast media; however, journalists claimed that pressure from politicians and organized criminal groups frequently resulted in self-censorship. Some journalists refrained from critical investigative reporting due to fear for their physical or job security. Journalists occasionally received offers of financial benefits in exchange for positive reporting or for abandoning an investigation. According to the AJK, government officials, as well as suspected criminals, verbally threatened journalists for perceived negative reporting. According to some editors, government agencies and corporations withdrew advertising from newspapers that published material critical of them.

Journalists complained that media owners and managers prevented them from publishing or broadcasting stories critical of the government, political parties, or particular officials due to the owners' preferences for, or connections with, the individuals concerned. In some cases owners reportedly threatened to dismiss journalists if they produced stories critical of the government and certain interest groups connected to the political establishment. Journalists complained that owners prevented them from producing stories on high-level government corruption.

Internet Freedom

The government did not restrict or disrupt access to the internet or censor online content, and there were no credible reports that the government monitored private online communications without appropriate legal authority.

As of November the Regulatory Authority of Electronic and Postal Communications reported that approximately 76 percent of all households had internet connections.

Academic Freedom and Cultural Events

There were no government restrictions on academic freedom or cultural events.

b. Freedom of Peaceful Assembly and Association

The constitution and law provide for the freedoms of assembly and association, and the government, EULEX, and KFOR generally respected these rights. The law on public gatherings requires organizers to inform police of protests 72 hours prior to the event. Police must notify protest organizers within 48 hours whether their application is accepted, otherwise the request was considered approved.

c. Freedom of Religion

See the Department of State's *International Religious Freedom Report* at www.state.gov/religiousfreedomreport/.

d. Freedom of Movement, Internally Displaced Persons, Protection of Refugees, and Stateless Persons

The law provides for freedom of movement within the country, foreign travel, emigration, and repatriation, and the government and EULEX generally respected these rights. Nevertheless, interethnic tensions, roadblocks placed by hardliners, and real and perceived security concerns restricted freedom of movement. Security concerns also limited the number of displaced Kosovo Serbs seeking to return.

Abuse of Migrants, Refugees, and Stateless Persons: On August 28, approximately 500 Kosovo-Albanian protesters blocked 150 displaced Kosovo-Serb pilgrims in three buses from reaching the ruins of a Serbian Orthodox monastery in Mushtishte/Musutiste to commemorate a religious holiday. Kosovo Police (KP) evacuated a local priest and his aide from the monastery and responded with tear gas and anti-riot measures to avoid injury to the pilgrims. The KP arrested 25 protesters for hurling rocks and bottles. Six police were injured. Minister for Communities and Returns Dalibor Jevtic told media that the names of potential returnees were placed on billboards before the visit to block their return. The KP escorted the pilgrims safely to the Visoki Decani Monastery.

The government cooperated with the Office of the UN High Commissioner for Refugees (UNHCR) and other humanitarian organizations in providing protection and assistance to internally displaced persons, refugees, returning refugees, asylum seekers, persons at risk of statelessness, and vulnerable minority communities.

On October 31, the Suhareke/Suva Reka municipal assembly passed a resolution against the return of Kosovo Serbs to the village of Mushtisht/Musutiste until the following conditions were met: return of missing villagers to their families, the Serbian government apologized for "killings, terror, and demolishment," and the perpetrators were brought before justice. Minister Jevtic said the resolution violated human rights, was unconstitutional, and was initiated by "property usurpers."

In-country Movement: Freedom of movement across the Austerlitz Bridge connecting Mitrovica/Mitrovice North and South was impeded despite agreement between the prime ministers of Kosovo and Serbia to open the bridge by June. Implementation of the agreement with the European Union began August 14 with the removal of the so-called "Peace Park" barrier; as of December 7, the process was still ongoing. The bridge remained blocked for vehicular traffic during the year, and in September foot traffic was rerouted to an alternate bridge while construction work was underway.

On October 29, local Kosovo Serbs in Mitrovica/Mitrovice North removed the last barricade (made of sand and gravel) located near an ethnically mixed Bosniak neighborhood. Kosovo Serbs had placed the barricade during July 2011 violence when the KP attempted to take over northern border crossings. On October 30, Kosovo Albanians removed the so-called "Adem Jashari square," which consisted of a concrete pipe with a Kosovo Liberation Army inscription and an Albanian national flag that had been placed in July 2014 in the center of an intersection in the Bosniak neighborhood.

Emigration and Repatriation: The return of the country's Ashkali, Egyptian, and Roma refugees from the war in 1999 remained a problem. Their institutional representatives believed that social prejudice prevented the return of nearly 400 Ashkalis, Egyptians, and Roma, displaced persons who told UNHCR they were ready to return from Macedonia and Montenegro. Nevertheless,

Gjakove/Djakovica Mayor Mimoza Kusari-Lila inaugurated 52 houses in January for Ashkali, Egyptian, and Roma returnees during the year.

The Ministry for Communities and Returns, with EU financial support, assisted 36 families comprising 197 displaced persons to return to the country, helping them with the purchase of livestock, farm equipment, and furniture, and providing assistance with obtaining legal documents and loans to start small enterprises. The ministry provided loans for income generating projects for returnees through its EU-funded community stabilization project to 119 individual and community projects, including 46 for the Roma, Ashkali, and Egyptian communities.

The ministry reported that as of October an interministerial commission it chaired to facilitate the return process had made no serious progress in establishing a special judicial panel to address displaced persons' claims to regain their previously seized property. The ministry also noted displaced persons still had difficulties in obtaining personal documents and cadastral services from municipalities.

Internally Displaced Persons (IDPs)

As of October, UNHCR estimated that 423 displaced persons resided in 29 collective centers (temporary, ad-hoc shelters) in the country.

According to UNHCR 116,151 persons from the country were displaced to other states in the region. Reportedly 8,367 displaced persons (2,104 families), primarily Kosovo Serbs, registered with UNHCR their interest in returning to the country. According to UNHCR, 307 individuals had returned through October 31. The government repeatedly invited all displaced persons to return to the country; however, obstacles persisted in terms of the allocation of land for housing reconstruction, limited funds, and a lack of socio-economic prospects. According to UNHCR, the lack of a detailed census and adequate profiling data left IDPs excluded from human rights protections and development plans.

The return process in some areas of the country continued to be marked by security incidents and by the host community's reluctance to accept minority returnees. No Kosovo Serb has yet returned to Gjakove/Djakovica. UNHCR observed limited opportunities for interaction between returnees and receiving communities as well as the returnees' lack of trust in law enforcement. In addition minority return was beset with security difficulties, and official obstruction in Istog/Istok, Kline/Klina, Mamushe/Mamusa, Mushtishte/Musutiste, and Mitrovica/Mitrovice North often discouraged returns. UNHCR reported that significant delays in providing voluntary returnees with reintegration assistance contributed to secondary displacement.

Protection of Refugees

Access to Asylum: The law provides for granting asylum or refugee status. The government has a system for providing protection to refugees, but, according to UNHCR, it lacked effective mechanisms and practices for identifying persons in need of international protection, as well as the countries of origin of undocumented individuals. According to the Ministry of Interior, none of the 957 asylum applications processed between 2008 and November resulted in the granting of refugee status, while only 13 individuals received subsidiary protection during this period. As of November there were 231 pending asylum applications. All asylum seekers departed the country before their claims were processed.

Authorities transferred to the asylum center all foreigners who were intercepted while illegally crossing borders and who subsequently sought asylum. Independent observers had access to the center. UNHCR reported that asylum seekers received accommodation, regular meals, and clothing provided by the center, as well as psychological assessment, counseling services, and legal aid. The lack of interpretation services in a number of languages remained a problem.

According to UNHCR the best interests of children were considered during the asylum process, but procedures for conducting such determinations were not in place. Reception facilities at the asylum center can host children, but the facility lacked standard operating procedures for the treatment of children seeking asylum.

In response to the emerging regional refugee crisis during the year, UNHCR and the International Organization for Migration (IOM) worked closely with the government to prepare an adequate response in the event of an influx of refugees and migrants. The planning process revealed that the country would require significant external resources to meet the needs of persons in transit and asylum seekers in case of such an influx. IOM noted that as of September, 4,872 of the country's citizens were repatriated from western European countries, the vast majority from Germany, where they had sought asylum. The Ministry of Interior worked with municipal authorities to provide support for these returnees, most of whom left the country in late 2014 and early 2015.

<u>Safe Country of Origin/Transit</u>: The Law on Asylum recognizes the safe country of origin concept under international law, but it has yet to be applied. According to UNHCR the country's definition of safe country of origin complies with EU standards.

<u>Freedom of Movement</u>: Per the country's law on foreigners, asylum seekers may not be detained unless charged with non-asylum-related crimes. UNHCR and the KRCT reported that foreigners held on charges in the detention center were treated humanely. The Department of Citizenship, Asylum, and Migration provided detainees with information on their rights in eight languages.

<u>Temporary Protection</u>: From independence in 2008 until November, the government provided subsidiary protection to 13 asylum seekers. The law provides for the granting of refugee status and subsidiary protection, and the government has established a protection system that was active and accessible.

Stateless Persons

Official figures on stateless persons were not available. The law contains no discriminatory provisions that might cause groups or individuals to be deprived of or denied citizenship. Children acquire citizenship from their parents or by virtue of birth in the country. The procedures provide for access to naturalization for those granted stateless or refugee status five years after the determination.

The law provides for issuance of travel documents to stateless persons. While laws relating to civil status permit them to register life events such as birth, marriage, and death, implementation varied among municipalities. The capacity to identify stateless persons and those with undetermined nationality remained inadequate.

As of November UNHCR assisted 408 unregistered ethnic Ashkalis, Egyptians, and Roma. Unregistered family members did not receive social assistance benefits and pension rights and could not register property titles or retain rights to inherited or transferred property. Children who were born of parents displaced outside the country and who entered with their readmitted parents often lacked documentation, including birth certificates, from their place of birth. Authorities acknowledged the problem but did not develop a systematic solution. In June 2015 the Civil Registration Agency of the Ministry of Internal Affairs promoted free birth registration and late registration by removing the expiration date that would have triggered fees or penalties for many registration services for ethnic Roma, Ashkalis, and Egyptians.

In August the Ministry of Interior reported 618 Ashkalis, Egyptians, and Roma were "legally invisible" due to their inability to provide evidence of their birth in the country. During the year the ministry's Civil Registration Agency provided birth certificates, IDs, and/or passports to 924 displaced persons from Kosovo in Montenegro.

Kosovo Serbs in four northern municipalities complained that they were not able to register births, marriages, or divorces, and thus obtain official Kosovo documents because their existing documents of life events were registered only under the government of Serbia's parallel system. During the year the government worked to establish civil registry offices in Kosovo-Serb majority areas in the north of the country, although they have struggled to open them and implement a new arrangement to permit registration. As of December 20, the Civil Registration Agency announced that Kosovo citizens in Zubin Potok, Leposavic/q, Zvecan, and Mitrovice/a could receive ID cards, passports, drivers licenses, and vehicle registrations.

Section 3. Freedom to Participate in the Political Process

The law provides citizens the ability to choose their government in free and fair periodic elections held by secret ballot based on universal and equal suffrage.

The Serbian government continued dismantling illegal parallel government structures in northern municipalities as part of the Brussels Dialogue implementation process between Serbia and the country, but some remained. Illegal parallel institutions also operated in Serbian and Gorani enclaves throughout the southern part of the country.

Elections and Political Participation

Recent Elections: The country's second national parliamentary elections since independence, and the first that included northern Kosovo, took place in 2014. International and independent observers evaluated the vote as generally free and fair.

Political Parties and Political Participation: Party affiliation played an important role in access to government services and social and employment opportunities. Clan loyalties also played an important role in political organizations. While minorities were overrepresented in parliament based on their overall share of the population, the country did not implement the public service law that called for 10 percent minority staffing at the local and national level. Ethnic-minority political parties criticized majority parties for not consulting on important issues.

Members of the opposition parties Vetevendosje, Nisma, and Alliance for the Future of Kosovo, used tear gas, pepper spray, and projectiles inside the legislature's plenary hall to attack members of the government and parliamentarians on numerous occasions during the year. They publicly stated that their intent was to block debate and the passage of legislation. In response authorities charged several members of parliament with weapons possession, causing general danger, and/or obstructing official persons in the performance of their duties.

Participation of Women and Minorities: No laws limit participation of women and minorities in the political process, and they did participate.

Section 4. Corruption and Lack of Transparency in Government

The law provides criminal penalties for corruption by officials, but the government did not implement the law effectively, with corruption remaining a serious problem. A lack of effective judicial oversight and general weakness in the rule of law contributed to the problem.

Corruption: The Kosovo Anticorruption Agency (ACA) and the Office of the Auditor General shared responsibility for combating government corruption. As of August the ACA received more than 89 reports alleging corruption, 81 of which concerned conflict of interest. ACA referred 24 of the cases it reviewed for prosecution and forwarded two involving 15 persons to police.

Convictions on corruption charges continued to represent a small proportion of those investigated and charged.

One of the largest anti-corruption raids in the country's history occurred on April 27, when the KP and EULEX searched 42 houses in connection with illegal real estate transactions. On October 25, special prosecutors filed two indictments in cases in which courts had previously made decisions to restitute property fraudulently confiscated by the former Yugoslav state. One case involved 22 persons charged with 46 counts of organized crime, money laundering, and other offenses. The other indictment was against 17 persons for participating in an organized criminal group suspected of money laundering and theft from a communally owned enterprise. Prosecutors alleged that the group has been active since 2006 and was led by former member of parliament Azem Syla, former president of the Pristina municipal court Nuhi Uka, as well as municipal court and privatization agency officials, attorneys, and several Kosovo Serbs from the Gracanica/Gracanice municipality. As of December 14, Syla was still in detention.

On July 18, Minister of Environment and Spatial Planning Ferid Agani resigned following his indictment related to a health-sector corruption case. On June 15, Minister Agani was indicted together with 63 others (including 44 doctors) in the so-called "stent case." Agani, formerly the minister of health, was charged with abuse of office concerning alleged violations of the public procurement law and ministry bylaws, specifically of improperly entering into agreements with private cardiology hospitals, paid by the government when public hospitals referred patients to them.

Financial Disclosure: The law obliges all senior public officials and their family members to declare their property and the origins of their property annually. Senior officials must also report changes in their property holdings when assuming or terminating their public service. The ACA administers this data, verifies disclosures, and publishes disclosures on its website. Based on a random sampling during the year, the agency reported that approximately 98 percent of officials declared their property and finances. Authorities may fine officials charged with minor breaches of the requirement or prohibit them from exercising public functions for up to one year. The ACA referred all charges against those who had not filed to prosecutors.

Public Access to Information: The law provides for public access to government information, but authorities did not effectively implement the law. Civil society organizations, which filed the majority of information requests, reported that government institutions rarely provided requested information or acknowledged the existence of particular documents requested.

Courts rarely accepted lawsuits against institutions that ignored document requests, and civil society organizations regarded this lack of consequences as an impediment to the law's effectiveness. On occasion officials reportedly denied document requests on grounds that the documents contained classified or secret information but would not reveal the name of the institution that classified the documents or the case number.

Section 5. Governmental Attitude Regarding International and Nongovernmental Investigation of Alleged Violations of Human Rights

A wide variety of domestic and international human rights groups operated, generally without government restriction, investigating and publishing their findings on human rights cases. The government was cooperative and somewhat responsive to their views.

Government Human Rights Bodies: The Ombudsperson Institution (OI) has authority to investigate allegations of human rights violations and abuse of government authority, and it acts as the national preventive mechanism against torture. The OI is the primary agency responsible for monitoring detention facilities; its seven field offices enabled it to maintain contact with all of the country's municipalities. Whenever its recommendations were not followed, the OI could bring cases to court against governmental bodies, including to the Constitutional Court. Based on powers granted by the assembly in 2015, as of December 14 the OI filed three amicus curiae briefs with the Constitutional Court. The OI can also make recommendations on the compatibility of laws and other sublegal or administrative acts, guidelines, and practices. The OI reported that the number of complaints it received during the first six months of the year was slightly less than for the same period in 2015; however, as of December it was unable to provide an exact tally.

Section 6. Discrimination, Societal Abuses, and Trafficking in Persons

Women

Rape and Domestic Violence: The law criminalizes rape but does not specifically address spousal rape. By law rape is punishable by two to 15 years in prison and statutory rape (sexual intercourse with a child younger than 16) by five to 20 years. Rape involving homicide is punishable by imprisonment from 10 years to life.

EULEX noted that courts often applied more lenient penalties than the legal minimum in rape cases, particularly in cases involving minors. EULEX found that courts rarely took steps to protect victims and witnesses, nor did they close hearings to the public as required by law.

According to the Kosovo Women's Network, more than two thirds of women had been victims of domestic violence, with 21 percent of respondents to a 2015 survey agreeing, "It is OK for a husband to hit his wife." Advocates maintained that such violence was underreported for reasons that included the social stigma associated with reporting such occurrences, a lack of trust in judicial institutions, traditional social attitudes in the male-dominated society, and a lack of viable options for victims.

The law treats domestic violence as a civil matter unless the victim suffers bodily harm. Failure to comply with a civil court's judgment relating to a domestic violence case is a criminal and prosecutable offense, although prosecutions for this offense were rare. According to victims' advocates, police responded according to established protocols to rape and domestic abuse allegations.

When victims pressed charges, police domestic violence units conducted investigations and transferred cases to prosecutors. The rate of prosecution was low due to societal factors as well as a backlog of cases in both civil and criminal courts. Advocates and court observers argued that prosecutors and judges favored family unification over victim protection, with protective orders sometimes allowing the perpetrator to remain in the family home while the case was pending. Advocates noted that victim confidentiality was often not respected, causing further harm. Sentences were frequently lenient, ranging from judicial reprimands to imprisonment from six months to five years.

The law permits individuals who feel threatened to petition for restraining orders, but violation of restraining orders seldom led to criminal charges. Courts rarely gave recidivists enhanced sentences as required by law.

On January 28, the Basic Court of Prizren issued an indictment for murder against Nebih Berisha, the spouse of Zejnepe Bytyqi Berisha from Suhareka/Suva Reka who was killed in October 2015. Berisha had been convicted in 2002 of domestic violence and, according to the Kosovo Women's Network, his wife had reported her husband for domestic violence eight times.

The Ministry of Labor and Social Welfare (MLSW) included a unit dedicated to family violence. The Kosovo Academy for Public Safety incorporated courses on human rights and work with victims of domestic violence, rape, and human trafficking into all of its basic training curricula for police cadets.

The government and international donors provided support to seven NGOs to assist children and female victims of domestic violence. There were 10 shelters for victims of domestic violence.

Through the President's National Council on Survivors, numerous officials participated in events dedicated to raising awareness of the need to provide support for individuals who suffered sexual assault related to the conflict in the late 1990s. The government took steps to acknowledge sexual survivors of wartime violence as a separate category in need of assistance but had not yet adopted a mechanism to provide them financial and psychological help, although the law and budget earmarked financial support for some survivors. In September, the MLSW issued a public call to form a verification commission to select beneficiaries, and on November 14, the ministry selected commission members. These survivors complained that EULEX prosecutors did not successfully prosecute any cases. The Ministry of Justice led a working group, including EULEX and the Special Prosecutor's Office, to prioritize cases, but no action was taken in any case.

Sexual Harassment: According to a report by the Kosovo Women's Network, the country has a number of laws considered applicable in relation to sexual harassment. In civil proceedings, the Law on Gender Equality, and the Law on Protection from Discrimination define sexual harassment. While the Criminal Code includes harassment, it does not contain a specific standard for sexual harassment; however, the code stipulates enhanced penalties for crimes against vulnerable victims, including victims of sexual abuse. Varying internal procedures and regulations for reporting sexual harassment hampered implementation of these laws.

According to women's rights organizations, sexual harassment on the job was common, and victims did not report it due to fear of physical retaliation or dismissal. Public awareness of sexual harassment remained low. In March the Forum of Women Judges and Prosecutors published the first "Bench-book," an overview of legal procedures for judges and prosecutors dealing with domestic violence, which included detailed guidance concerning factors that could be considered as aggravating ones, and recognized victims of domestic violence as vulnerable victims.

Reproductive Rights: Couples and individuals have the right to decide the number, spacing, and timing of their children, manage their reproductive health, and have access to the information and means to do so, free from discrimination, coercion, or violence. The government generally respected reproductive rights, but poor, marginalized, and illiterate communities often had limited access to information, and public health facilities provided limited treatment for sexually transmitted infections.

<u>Discrimination</u>: The law provides the same legal status and rights for women as for men. The law requires equal pay for equivalent work. The traditionally lower status of women within the family affected their treatment within the legal system.

The law stipulates that the partners in marriage and civil unions have equal rights to own and inherit property, but men commonly inherited family property and only 8 percent of women owned land. According to laws regulating inheritance and family matters, upon death the assets of the deceased were to be shared equally among the spouse and children, with second-degree relatives inheriting only if all first-degree relatives were deceased. In the event of a will, gender could not be used as a condition to limit inheritance. In rare instances Kosovo-Albanian widows, particularly in rural areas, risked losing custody of their children due to a custom requiring children and property to pass to the deceased father's family while the widow returned to her birth family.

Relatively few women occupied upper-level management positions in business, police, or government. Women constituted 45 percent of the public-sector workforce in 2015. According to the Ministry of Trade and Industry, women owned approximately 20 percent of all registered businesses (see section 7.d). A recent study by the think tank Democracy for Development found that only one in 10 women in the country were employed.

<u>Gender-biased Sex Selection</u>: According to the Kosovo Agency for Statistics, in 2012, the date of the last census, the male to female gender ratio at birth was 110.7 to 100. According to the UN Children's Fund (UNICEF), the government did not take steps to address this imbalance, such as by regulating private clinics, or helping to increase women's social status.

Children

<u>Birth Registration</u>: Children acquire citizenship from their parents or by virtue of birth in the country. According to the Kosovo Agency for Statistics' Multiple Indicator Cluster Survey (MICS) covering 2013-14, the births of 88 percent of children younger than five were registered. Lack of registration generally did not affect a child's ability to receive elementary education or health care, but UNICEF indicated it could adversely affect access to social assistance, particularly for repatriated children. Children who were not registered were considered stateless.

<u>Child Abuse</u>: Child abuse was a problem. In 2015 UNICEF found that 30 percent of children in the country, and 40 percent of ethnic Romani, Ashkali, and Egyptian

children, were victims of abuse. UNICEF believed that the abuse was underreported due to low levels of public awareness of child abuse, lack of services for victims, and authorities' limited capacity to identify, report, and refer cases of abuse. According to MICS, family members subjected 61 percent of children under the age of 14 to "psychological aggression" or physical punishment. According to a 2012 Global Initiative to End All Corporal Punishment report, more than 80 percent of respondents from the country said it was justified to hit a child for stealing. Fifty-nine percent of children and 80 percent of parents said that teachers were violent towards children.

<u>Early and Forced Marriage</u>: The law allows persons to marry at age 16. Child marriage was rare but continued in certain ethnic communities, including the Roma, Ashkalis, Egyptians, and Gorani. According to a separate MICS report that focused on these communities, approximately 12 percent of children, mostly girls, married before the age of 15. The Ministry of Local Government Administration and the Agency for Gender Equality in the prime minister's office conducted informational campaigns to discourage early marriage.

<u>Sexual Exploitation of Children</u>: The minimum age of consensual sex is 16. Statutory rape is a criminal offense, which, depending on circumstances and the age of the victim, is punishable by five years to life in prison. The law prohibits possession, production, and distribution of child pornography. Persons who produce, use, or involve a child in making or producing pornography may receive sentences of one to five years. Distribution, promotion, transmission, offer, or display of child pornography is punishable by six months to five years. Possession or procurement of child pornography is punishable by a fine or imprisonment of up to three years. As of November 10, KP conducted five investigations. Prosecutors indicted two persons during the year in one case of child pornography.

<u>International Child Abductions</u>: The country is not a party to the 1980 Hague Convention on the Civil Aspects of International Child Abduction. For further information see the Department of State's *Annual Report on International Parental Child Abduction* at travel.state.gov/content/childabduction/en/legal/compliance.html.

Anti-Semitism

Approximately 50 Jewish persons resided in the country, according to the Jewish Community of Kosovo. On November 15, the Simon Wiesenthal Center in France issued a public letter to President Hashim Thaci that criticized the ready availability in the country of notorious anti-Semitic literature, allegedly translated into Albanian and published in Egypt by the Muslim Brotherhood. The Wiesenthal Center said it had lodged a complaint with the Ministry of Interior. On November 30, President Thaci announced a decision to ban the sale and distribution of anti-Semitic books. As of December 14, no administrative action was taken to implement this decision.

Trafficking in Persons

See the Department of State's *Trafficking in Persons Report* at www.state.gov/j/tip/rls/tiprpt/.

Persons with Disabilities

The constitution and law prohibit discrimination against persons with physical, sensory, intellectual, and mental disabilities in employment, education, transportation, health care, in the judicial system, or other state services. The government did not effectively enforce these provisions, and persons with disabilities suffered discrimination (see section 7.d.).

Persons with disabilities were eligible for small assistance payments from the government. The MLSW was responsible for protecting the rights of persons with disabilities and had sole responsibility for managing these payments and pensions for such persons. According to HandiKos a disability rights organization, health, social assistance, rehabilitation, and assistive devices for persons with disabilities remained insufficient, and physical access to public institutions remained difficult even after the implementation of bylaws on building and administrative support.

The MLSW has not yet addressed the issue of more than 1,000 deaf individuals who were removed from the disability pension scheme in 2013. The Law on Paraplegic and Tetraplegic Persons was adopted in May, and enters into force in 2017. As of November, the government had no budget for its implementation. The National Disability Council appointed the president of the Kosovo Disability Forum as the council's co-chair.

According to the EU's *Kosovo 2016 Report*, health and social assistance for persons with disabilities remained insufficient, and physical access to public institutions remained a challenge. The EU also expressed concern about the lack of personal assistants for children with disabilities. According to the report, the government did not effectively implement the Strategy for the Rights of People with Disabilities (2013-2023). As of November 9, it had not drafted a new action plan for 2017-2019. HandiKos reported that persons with spinal cord injuries, muscular dystrophy, Down syndrome, and multiple sclerosis lacked access to essential services, social assistance, and employment. Access to public buildings and public transport remained problematic throughout the country.

The Law on Mental Health regulates the commitment of persons to psychiatric or social care facilities and protects their rights within such institutions. The labor and health ministries had separate mandates for treating persons with mental disabilities. Although the Law on Mental Health entered into force in December 2015, as of November bylaws were not approved and the law was not implemented. The Ministry of Health and the Ministry of Labor each operated nine community homes for people with mental disabilities. The KRCT described mental health facilities as substandard. The country's facilities did not have appropriate staff, such as psychiatrists, psychologists, social workers, physiotherapists, and other technical experts.

The KRCT reported that several persons with mental disabilities were in detention without any legal basis but noted courts were reviewing some cases. The KRCT also observed that facilities and treatment for inmates with disabilities remained substandard (see section 1.c.).

National/Racial/Ethnic Minorities

Ethnic minorities, including Serb, Romani, Ashkali, Egyptian, Turkish, Bosniak, Gorani, Croat, and Montenegrin communities, faced varying levels of institutional and societal discrimination in employment (see section 7.d), education, social services, language use, freedom of movement, the right to return to their homes (for displaced persons), and other basic rights.

The prime minister's Office of Community Affairs (OCA) noted discrimination in public-sector employment in almost all local and national institutions. There were no legal remedies to address these concerns.

Romani, Ashkali, and Egyptian communities experienced pervasive social and economic discrimination. They often lacked access to basic hygiene, medical care, and education, and were heavily dependent on humanitarian aid for subsistence. The OCA found language and religious discrimination against Kosovo Serbs were among reasons inhibiting their return and survival in the country.

Incidents against Kosovo Serbs persisted, particularly in the Peje/Pec, Istog/Istok, and Kline/Klina regions. In the first eight months of the year, there were more than 111 incidents involving thefts, break-ins, verbal harassment, and damage to the property of Kosovo Serbs and the Serbian Orthodox Church. Ethnic Albanians occasionally used violence to prevent ethnic Serbs from attending religious services in certain areas (see section 2.d.). After the St. Vitus Serbian Orthodox celebration on June 28, police reported an unidentified assailant threw two Molotov cocktails at a police-escorted convoy of displaced Kosovo-Serb pilgrims visiting from Serbia. An unidentified individual also threw stones at another van of pilgrims in the Mitrovica/e region.

A memorial plaque placed at the outskirts of Rahovec/Orahovac to commemorate two Kosovo-Serb journalists who went missing in 1998, was vandalized during the year for the fifth time since 2012. The Association of Kosovo-Serb Journalists condemned the incident and blamed the government for failing to act upon information it provided to help locate missing persons. In August, President Thaci visited two memorials dedicated to Kosovo-Serb victims. One of the monuments was subsequently defaced with Albanian-nationalist graffiti.

On July 19, the NGO Center for Peace and Tolerance (CPT) criticized the KP, EULEX, and the EU Office in Kosovo for failing to prevent, properly register, and adequately investigate interethnic incidents, primarily perpetrated against Kosovo Serbs. CPT asserted that victims did not report crimes due to a lack of trust in public-sector institutions. Deputy Prime Minister Branimir Stojanovic called for an increase in the number of Kosovo Serbs on the police force, noting a reduction in some areas. As of November Kosovo Serbs represented 12.7 percent of KP's uniformed officers (991 of 7,821). During KP's March basic training class, Kosovo Serbs made up 12.2 percent of the 287 graduates. In response to Kosovo-Serb community safety concerns, the KP promoted a Kosovo Serb to the rank of Lieutenant and appointed him to serve as the Gorazdevac Police Substation Commander in a Kosovo-Serb majority area.

In January the secretariat of the Kosovo Judicial Council decided to close the last court liaison offices in Gracanica/e, which provided legal assistance to minority communities, including refugees and displaced persons. Following the closure, there was no free legal aid provided by the country specifically for the Kosovo-Serb community, although an EU project funded some NGOs who provided grant-based services.

Crimes were reported against the ethnic Bosniak communities in the Mitrovice/Mitrovica, Peje/Pec, and the Prizren regions, including targeted thefts, threats, assaults, property damage, forced prostitution, and the planting of an explosive device. Similar crimes were reported against the Gorani community in the Dragash/Dragas area. There were also attacks reported against members of the Romani, Ashkali, and Egyptian communities in the Peje/Pec, Ferizaj/Urosevac, and Mitrovice/Mitrovica North and South municipalities. These included targeted thefts, kidnapping, and trafficking of Ashkali women. While most of these crimes went unpunished, on October 24, authorities broke up a human trafficking ring allegedly led by a Kosovo Ashkali minor woman.

The security environment in the north of the country remained unpredictable. In July a Kosovo Bosniak sustained bodily injuries and required medical care after being assaulted by two unknown assailants in the ethnically mixed village of Suhodoll/Suvi Do. The victim had just completed prayers at a local mosque. There were also several cases of business, school, and vehicle arson, explosions, theft, and property damage. Although police indicated that most incidents were internal to the Kosovo-Serb community and not ethnically motivated, there were ethnic confrontations between young Kosovo Albanians and Kosovo Serbs near the Austerlitz Bridge.

Discussions regarding the reconstruction of houses damaged during or after the war in the ethnically mixed Kroi i Vitakut/Brdjani neighborhood continued. The Ministry for Communities and Returns, the Ministry of Local Government Administration, and neighborhood representatives met periodically but made little progress. In accordance with the August 2015 dialogue agreement, the Mitrovica/Mitrovice North and Mitrovice/Mitrovica South mayors and the EU continued to discuss the administrative lines between the municipalities, but they did not reach agreement.

The language commissioner monitored and reported on the implementation of legislation that conferred equal status to the country's two official languages, Albanian and Serbian, as well as official languages used at the local level, including Bosnian, Romani, and Turkish. The commissioner told the media in March that the implementation of the country's languages legislation was insufficient, resulting in the absence or incorrect translation of official documents.

Although government institutions may incur fines for not respecting the language requirements, there were no reports of fines. The commissioner lacked direct enforcement powers. Most government institutions failed to provide equal amounts of information online in languages other than Albanian. Kosovo Serbs complained that translations into Serbian of laws, other official documents, and government websites were inadequate, and sometimes conflicting, even though the Albanian and Serbian versions of laws have equal standing. The commissioner told the media that the country's constitution had 930 translation errors between the two official languages.

Minority groups praised amendments to administrative rulings that permitted Bosniaks, Roma, and Turks to have identity documents issued in their own languages. Representatives of the Turkish community expressed dissatisfaction with implementation of the official languages law, especially in Prizren municipality, where Turkish is an official language. Officials maintained translations of street names and personal documentation were missing or poorly done. Similar shortcomings occurred in municipalities where the Bosnian and Romani languages have official status.

The employment of minorities in public institutions remained limited and generally confined to lower levels of the government. According to a report from the Kosovo Democratic Institute think tank, only 6.2 percent of the government's civil service employees were non-Albanian minorities, although the law on civil service mandates that 10 percent of the employees at the local and national levels be minorities. The report noted that the members of Ashkali, Egyptian, Gorani, and Roma communities were "visibly underrepresented" at all civil service levels. The report also stated the government lacked an effective mechanism for monitoring levels of minority employment in public institutions.

On September 25, the Ministry of Justice published a list of candidates who passed the bar examination, including the five Kosovo-Serb candidates who intended to be integrated into the Kosovo justice system and work in Mitrovica/Mitrovice North Basic Court in accordance with the Dialogue Agreement on Justice. Bosniak community representatives complained their members were not allowed to apply for positions as prosecutors and judges in the north of the country, in violation, they claimed, of the constitution. In July, eight Bosniaks appealed to the Kosovo Prosecutorial Council and the Kosovo Judiciary Council about the decision to reject their applications for court positions in the north of the country. Four petitioners received negative responses and filed cases with the Independent Civil Service Oversight Board.

The law requires equal conditions for schoolchildren regardless of their mother tongue and provides minority students with the right to public education in their native languages through secondary school. This law was not enforced, with Kosovo's Bosniak, Croat, Gorani, Montenegrin, Roma, and Turk leaders noting that their communities lacked textbooks and other materials.

The Ministry of Education, Science, and Technology (MEST) and several international organizations reported school enrollment was lowest among the country's non-Serb minority communities. Romani, Ashkali, and Egyptian children suffered from lower registration rates, higher dropout rates, and poor levels of performance. In most cases, such as in the Pristina and Prizren municipalities, elementary school attendance levels reportedly continued to decrease, resulting in registration of only one Bosniak child in the single elementary school in the Pristina Bosnian language program.

On June 3, MEST issued the country's first administrative ruling formally to set aside 12 percent of admissions, dormitories, and stipends for minorities in undergraduate and graduate programs at seven public universities. On September 21, MEST amended a 2013 ruling to permit the University of Prizren to register students in BA programs in elementary education, pre-elementary education, and information technology and telecommunication in the Bosnian and Turkish languages. Prior to this change, Kosovo Bosnian and Turkish graduates in these fields were unable to use their diplomas; this decision retroactively recognized their diplomas.

All minorities complained that the government did not provide sufficient textbooks for non-Albanian-speaking students at any educational level. According to MEST, many of the schools teaching in Serbian imported textbooks from Serbia that did not conform to provisions of the domestic curriculum. On June 9, the ministry renewed its September 2015 decision banning the importation of Serbian textbooks after Serbia did not allow MEST-sponsored Albanian-language books for students in Serbia's Presevo Valley. This ban effectively blocked the importation of all books, including non-textbooks from Serbia.

The University of Pristina, the country's largest university, taught classes only in Albanian. Based on MEST's June 3 administrative instruction, the University of Pristina and the country's six other public universities offered the first-round entrance examinations to students in minority languages, as required by law.

The number of registered minority students in the first round was significantly higher than in 2015--from several dozen to more than a hundred.

Kosovo Bosniaks praised the implementation of legislation that allowed the country's Bosniaks, Roma, and Turks to obtain identity documents in their own languages. Representatives of the Turkish community expressed dissatisfaction with overall implementation of the official languages law. Representatives of these communities claimed that translation of the official correspondence was not automatically available in the Bosnian and Turkish languages in the Prizren municipality, as provided by law. Translation of street names and personal documentation in Prizren was missing or poorly done. Similar shortcomings occurred in municipalities where the Bosnian and Romani languages had official status. The Gracanica/Gracanice municipality employed two Romani-language translators.

The government's nonrecognition of diplomas issued by the University in Mitrovica/Mitrovice North (UNM), which operated under the government of Serbia's system, was a key impediment to employment of Kosovo Serbs and other minorities within governmental institutions. Government officials discussed with Serbian counterparts the mutual recognition of diplomas through the Kosovo-Serbia Dialogue on September 29.

Acts of Violence, Discrimination, and Other Abuses Based on Sexual Orientation and Gender Identity.

The constitution and law prohibit direct or indirect discrimination based on sexual orientation and gender identity in employment, health care, and education.

When the motivation for a crime was based on gender, sexual orientation, or perceived affinity of the victim with persons who are targets of such hostility, the law considers motivation to be an aggravating circumstance.

An Advisory and Coordinating Group consisting of representatives of eight ministries, the Office of Good Governance, and three NGOs cooperated to protect and promote the rights of the LGBTI community. This group met twice during the year but as of December did not complete the country's first National Action Plan for LGBT rights. The group lacked executive authority to implement its decisions. As of December 7, no monitoring had occurred to track the implementation of the group's decisions.

Government officials signaled support for LGBTI rights by sponsoring and attending numerous public events, such as the third annual pride walk on the International Day against Homophobia and Biphobia, which was the largest in the country's history. President Thaci became the country's first president to participate in the walk.

According to human rights NGOs, the LGBTI community faced overt discrimination in employment, housing, determination of statelessness, and access to education and health care. The NGOs said societal pressure persuaded most LGBTI persons to conceal their sexual orientation or gender identity. NGOs reported that discrimination against LGBTI individuals often went unreported, alleging that police were insensitive to the needs of their community.

On September 26, the court sentenced two defendants for attacking two members of the LGBTI community who had been distributing HIV prevention materials in Ferizaj/Urosevac just prior to the attack. The court sentenced one defendant to five months in prison for inciting hatred, as well as assault. This was the first conviction in the country's history for a hate crime perpetrated against members of the LGBTI community. The NGO Center for Social Group Development, however, expressed concern that the court did not cite sexual orientation as the motivating factor.

According to NGOs, as of October LGBTI persons had reported 19 hate crimes since 2012, including five during the year.

In June a German tourist was allegedly attacked because of his sexual orientation, in a case that police and prosecutors consider a hate crime. In July a landlord allegedly attacked his tenants, gay couple. According to the couple, the landlord had threatened them in the presence of police, but police did not arrest him. The case was reported to the ombudsman; however, LGBTI groups criticized the ombudsman's lack of response. The prosecution did not file an indictment.

HIV and AIDS Social Stigma

While there were no confirmed reports of official discrimination against persons with HIV/AIDS during the year, anecdotal reports of such discrimination persisted.

Other Societal Violence or Discrimination

There were no so-called honor killings reported during the year.

Section 7. Worker Rights

a. Freedom of Association and the Right to Collective Bargaining

The law provides for the right of workers to form and join independent unions, bargain collectively, and conduct legal strikes. The law prohibits antiunion discrimination and the violation of any individual's labor rights due to his or her union activities. The law requires reinstatement of workers fired for union activity, including in essential services. The law applies equally to all individuals working in the public and private sectors, including documented migrants and domestic servants.

Authorities did not effectively enforce the labor law, which includes regulations, and administrative instructions that govern employment relations, including rights to freedom of association and collective bargaining. According to the Association of Independent Labor Unions in Kosovo (BSPK), resources, inspections, and remediation were inadequate, and penalties insufficient. As of July the Ministry of Labor and Social Work's (MLSW) Labor Inspectorate issued 56 fines ranging from no monetary penalty to 35,000 euros ($38,500). The BSPK described these fines as insufficient to deter violations. Administrative and judicial procedures were circuitous and subject to lengthy delays or appeals.

According to the BSPK, the government and employers in the country generally respected the right to form and join unions in both the public and private sectors. Political party interference in trade union organizations and individual worker rights remained an issue. According to union officials, workers in the public sector commonly faced mistreatment, including sexual harassment and the loss of employment, based on their political party affiliation. Employers did not always respect the rights of worker organizations to bargain collectively. The BSPK reported that many private sector employers essentially ignored the country's labor laws. The BSPK reported continued difficulty in establishing unions due to employer interference in workers' associations and unions, particularly in the banking, construction, and hotel sectors. Representatives from these sectors told the BSPK anonymously that employers used intimidation to prevent the establishment of unions. The Labor Inspectorate reported receiving no formal complaints of discrimination against employees who tried to join unions during the year. The BSPK claimed the inspectorate was not fully functional due to budgetary and staffing shortfalls.

b. Prohibition of Forced or Compulsory Labor

The law prohibits all forms of forced or compulsory labor, but forced child labor occurred during the year (see section 7.c.).

Government resources, including remediation, were insufficient to bring about compliance, identify and protect victims, and investigate claims of forced or compulsory labor. There were no investigations, prosecutions, or convictions of forced labor due, according to the Labor Inspectorate, to inadequate resources. Penalties ranged from five to 12 years' imprisonment and a fine of up to 500,000 euros ($550,000) and were sufficiently stringent compared with those for other serious crimes. As of September authorities did not remove any victims from forced labor.

Also see the Department of State's *Trafficking in Persons Report* at www.state.gov/j/tip/rls/tiprpt/.

c. Prohibition of Child Labor and Minimum Age for Employment

The minimum age for contractual employment is 15, provided the employment is not harmful or prejudicial to school attendance. If the work is likely to jeopardize the health, safety, or morals of a young person, the legal minimum age is 18. In 2013, the government agreed with the International Labor Organization on protections from hazardous labor for children in agriculture, street labor, construction, and the exploitation of natural resources. Regulations forbid exploitation of children in the workplace, including forced or compulsory labor. The government maintained a committee for prevention and elimination of child labor to intervene in cases of forced or hazardous labor. The committee was constrained by limited resources. The government also maintained a National Authority against Trafficking in Persons that investigated cases of children trafficked for labor.

Inspectors immediately notify employers when finding minors working in hazardous conditions. As of June, Municipal Social Work Offices (MSWO) reported only three cases of minors working in hazardous conditions to the MLSW; but it had no information on whether the children returned to school. Two of the minors were begging, and one worked at a waste disposal site. The MLSW noted that MSWO halted its reporting of cases of minors working in hazardous conditions to the MLSW. This poor coordination among the country's institutions and the lack of a centralized repository resulted in considerable underreporting of actual cases. During the year the MLSW established a new reporting tool that would allow for simultaneous reporting to the MLSW and MSWO. As of

November 10, the tool was not operational, and the MLSW could not provide accurate numbers for the year.

Under the labor code, inspectors may fine employers from 100 euros ($110) to 10,000 euros ($11,000) for subjecting a worker to hazardous working conditions. Fines were double for offenses committed against a minor. Enforcement was poor due to inadequate training and resources. The law provides additional penalties for employers and families that engage children in labor practices or fail to meet their parental obligations resulting in the illegal employment of a minor. The law permits authorities to remove a child from the home if that is determined to be in the best interests of a child.

The Coalition for Protection of Children (KOMF) reported that children working in the farming and mining sectors encountered hazards associated with operating farm equipment and extracting ore from hard-to-reach areas underground. The KOMF also reported that the total number of child beggars remained unknown. While most children were rarely their families' main wage earners, child labor contributed substantially to some family incomes.

Young children in rural areas often assisted their families in agricultural labor, typically including work during school hours. Urban children often worked in a variety of unofficial construction and retail jobs, such as selling newspapers, cigarettes, food, and telephone cards on the street. Some children also engaged in physical labor, such as transportation of goods.

See the Department of Labor's *Findings on the Worst Forms of Child Labor* at www.dol.gov/ilab/reports/child-labor/findings/.

d. Discrimination with Respect to Employment and Occupation

The law prohibits any discrimination, based on race, color, sex, religion, age, family status, political opinion, national extraction or social origin, language, gender identity, disability, health status, pregnancy, genetic inheritance, or trade union membership that has the effect of nullifying or impairing equality of opportunity, treatment in employment, or occupation capacity building. The law specifically prohibits discrimination based on gender, or gender identity, and applies to access to employment, self-employment, and choice of occupation. The prohibitions include discrimination in promotion and recruitment conditions in any branch of activity and at all levels of the professional hierarchy. Fines in cases of discrimination are between 500 and 10,000 euros ($550 and $11,000). The law does not protect against discrimination based on HIV status or other communicable diseases. According to the NGO GAP Institute, the penalties were adequate, but the number of labor inspectors was insufficient for the system to function properly, and therefore the government was unable to enforce the labor law effectively.

Discrimination in employment and occupation occurred across sectors with respect to sex, gender, gender identity, disability, and minority status (see section 6). During the year the BSPK received reports from labor unions and individuals also claiming discrimination based on age and family status. BSPK claimed to be the only entity where workers reported discrimination due to fear of employer retribution. The BSPK noted that employment often depended on the employee's political status and affiliation. The BSPK also stated that due to high unemployment, employees were reluctant to report discrimination, fearing retaliation by their employer. Most often employees addressed their work-related matters internally and informally with their employers. The BSPK also reported instances of employers discriminating against female candidates in employment interviews, and illegally firing women for being pregnant or requesting maternity leave.

By law foreigners must obtain work permits prior to seeking work in the country. According to the Labor Inspectorate, there were no reports of foreign workers denied work permits, and there were no reports of violation of foreign workers' rights during the year.

e. Acceptable Conditions of Work

The government-set minimum wage was 130 euros ($143) per month for employees younger than 35, and 170 euros ($187) per month for those 35 and older. For those earning less than minimum wage, the law provides monthly benefits of up to 120 euros ($132) for eligible families and up to 40 euros ($44) monthly for individuals. Families and individuals could also receive discounts on up to 400 kilowatt-hours of electricity and free health care.

The law provides for a standard 40-hour workweek, requires rest periods, limits the number of regular hours worked to 12 hours per day, limits overtime to 20 hours per week and 40 hours per month, requires payment of a premium for overtime work, and prohibits excessive compulsory overtime. The law provides for 20 days' paid leave per year for employees and 12 months of partially paid maternity leave. The labor law sets health and safety standards for workplaces and governs all industries in the country.

Labor inspectors, from the MLSW, were responsible for enforcing all labor standards, including those pertaining to wages, hours, and occupational safety and health. The MLSW's 51 labor inspectors review provisions of the country's labor code pertaining to contractual labor, health, and safety standards. Unions considered the number of inspectors insufficient to monitor the formal and informal sectors effectively. As of October these inspectors conducted 5,866 random and planned inspections. The Labor Inspectorate advised employers on improvements to comply with workplace regulations and of breaches that could bring about official sanctions. As of October the Labor Inspectorate issued 717 warnings for various violations of labor standards and levied 94 additional fines of up to 35,000 euros ($38,500) for failure to correct cited violations. As of October the inspectorate conducted 359 inspections based on employee complaints against their employers. The Labor Inspectorate received 150 complaints against fines and warnings issued by the labor inspectors. The Labor Inspectorate resolved these complaints in 15 to 60 days. It estimated it would need 150 inspectors to adequately monitor employers or have a measurable impact on labor problems. The inspectorate considered the financial penalties insufficient to discourage violations.

According to the Labor Inspectorate and the BSPK, the labor code is comprehensive and its provisions on work hours are adequate for the equal protection of public and private sector workers. According to the BSPK, the government's lack of enforcement stemmed from a paucity of unionized workers as well as resource and capacity limitations of the Labor Inspectorate.

The Ministry of Labor continued efforts to compile amendments to the labor code, needed to implement the government-sponsored Collective Contract. The Collective Contract establishes the rights and obligations of the employer and the employee, including provisions on work hours, night work, annual leave, maternity leave, job safety, and employee health benefits. The contract also includes all of the protections in the labor laws and applies to all workers in the informal as well as formal economies. Observers noted that the agreement was intended to reduce the size of the informal economy by penalizing employers who do not register employees.

According to the BSPK, employers failed to abide by official labor standards that provided equal standards of protection to public and private sector workers. The BSPK reported a lack of government oversight and enforcement, particularly with regard to the standard workweek and compulsory and unpaid overtime. Many individuals worked long hours in the private sector as "at-will" employees, without employment contracts, regular pay, or contributions to their pensions. The BSPK reported that employers ignored legal provisions and fired workers without cause in violation of the law and refused to respect workers holidays. As of July the Labor Inspectorate received 229 formal complaints of violations of workers' rights in the public and private sectors. Women's rights organizations reported that sexual abuse and harassment occurred on the job but went unreported due to fear of expulsion or retaliation.

While the law provides for the protection of employees' health and working conditions, private and public institutions failed at times to comply. The Labor Inspectorate and BSRK officials reported difficulties in obtaining accurate information about compliance, because workers rarely disclosed the problems due to fear of losing their jobs. The Labor Inspectorate reported five workplace fatalities and 25 serious workplace accidents as of July.

No law specifically permits an employee to leave work due to a dangerous work situation, but the law requires every employer to provide adequate work conditions for all employees based upon job requirements. According to the MLSW, informal employer-employee arrangements may address when and whether an employee may leave work due to dangerous work situations. The country's institutions did not track these arrangements. According to experts, violations of wage, overtime, and occupational health and safety standards were common for men and women, as well as foreign migrant workers, particularly those who faced hazardous or exploitative working conditions.